THINK SPEAK ACT KINDLY

366 Easy and Free Ideas You can Use to Create a Kinder World...Starting Today!

The Love and Kindness
Project Foundation

(BW Version)

When's the perfect time to get started
practicing kindness?

RIGHT NOW!

INTRODUCTION

Kindness is a practice. The more we practice, the easier it gets to think kindly, speak kindly and act kindly.

That's why this book is divided into three sections:

Think Kindly has ideas you can use to think kind and positive thoughts - about yourself and others.

Speak Kindly has ideas for words and phrases you can use to speak kindly to others - and to yourself!

Act Kindly has ideas for easy, free everyday acts of kindness that you can do - and help others do as well!

How to use this book to start - and deepen - your kindness practice:

Every morning choose one page to focus on for the day. You can go in order, or choose any page you'd like! It's up to you!

Read the idea and think about what you can do.

Hint: To make it easy to remember, take a picture

of the page and make it your phone and computer screensaver!

Every evening, fill in what you did to Think Kindly, Speak Kindly or Act Kindly, how it made others feel, and how it made you feel!

Then, share your daily kindness practice with your family members and friends...and post on social media. Because the more each of us Thinks Kindly, Speaks Kindly and Acts Kindly, the kinder world we'll create for all of us!

As I always say, "No matter who we are, where we live, or what we believe in, as long as we think kindly, speak kindly and act kindly towards others and ourselves, the world will be a better place!"

Thank you for practicing kindness!

Karyn and all Your Friends at The Love and Kindness Project Foundation

ACT KINDLY

Our thoughts create the
words we speak...

What I did: _______________________

What happened: _______________________

How I felt: _______________________

What I did: _______________________

What happened: _______________________

How I felt: _______________________

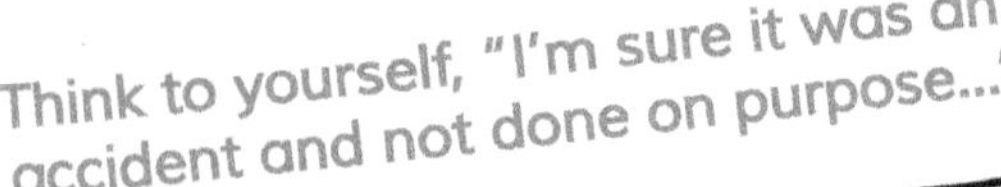

What I did: ______________________________
____

What happened: ______________________________
____

How I felt: ______________________________
____
____

What I did: ______________________________
____

What happened: ______________________________
____

How I felt: ______________________________
____

loveandkindnessproject.org

Take three deep breaths before
responding if you feel upset or angry.

What I did:

What happened:

How I felt:

Write as long a list as you can about
things that make you happy!

What I did:

What happened:

How I felt:

If you are upset with someone, think about something fun you did with them in the past.

What I did: ___________________________________

____

What happened: _______________________________

____

How I felt: __________________________________

____

____

Look through an old photo album with pictures from a fun vacation.

What I did: ___________________________________

____

What happened: _______________________________

____

How I felt: __________________________________

____

loveandkindnessproject.org

What I did:

What happened:

How I felt:

What I did:

What happened:

How I felt:

What I did:

What happened:

How I felt:

What I did:

What happened:

How I felt:

loveandkindnessproject.org

What I did:

What happened:

How I felt:

What I did:

What happened:

How I felt:

What I did: ___________________________

____

What happened: ___________________________

____

How I felt: ___________________________

____

____

What I did: ___________________________

____

What happened: ___________________________

____

How I felt: ___________________________

____

     loveandkindnessproject.org

Smile! Even if you don't feel like it!

What I did:

What happened:

How I felt:

Chat with a positive-minded friend!

What I did:

What happened:

How I felt:

Start a gratitude journal!

What I did: __________________________

____

What happened: ______________________

____

How I felt: __________________________

____

____

Go for a run or do another form of exercise you like!

What I did: __________________________

____

What happened: ______________________

____

How I felt: __________________________

____

loveandkindnessproject.org

What I did:

What happened:

How I felt:

What I did:

What happened:

How I felt:

Do some gardening!

What I did:

What happened:

How I felt:

Write an 'I forgive you note' to yourself.

What I did:

What happened:

How I felt:

   loveandkindnessproject.org

Look at your hands and tell yourself
all the wonderful things they can do!

What I did:

What happened:

How I felt:

Plant seeds!

What I did:

What happened:

How I felt:

Think about the worst joke you've
ever heard and just laugh!

What I did:
____
____

What happened:
____
____

How I felt:
____
____
____

Do jumping jacks every time
you have a negative thought!

What I did:
____
____

What happened:
____
____

How I felt:
____
____

   loveandkindnessproject.org

Make a list of all the 'other' possible reasons why something could have happened that aren't the negative one you are assuming.

What I did:

What happened:

How I felt:

Write your negative thoughts down and throw them away.

What I did:

What happened:

How I felt:

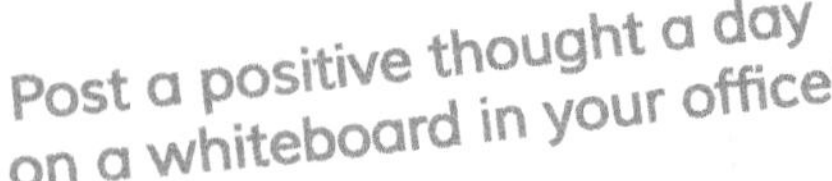

What I did:

What happened:

How I felt:

Wear a Love and Kindness Bracelet and
look at it regularly to reorient yourself
towards kind thoughts !

What I did:

What happened:

How I felt:

loveandkindnessproject.org

Create a playlist of positive music!

What I did:

What happened:

How I felt:

If you think an unkind thought, immediately change it to a kind one!

What I did:

What happened:

How I felt:

What I did:

What happened:

How I felt:

What I did:

What happened:

How I felt:

 loveandkindnessproject.org

Set aside 15 minutes a day to deliberately practice thinking kind thoughts!

What I did:

What happened:

How I felt:

Ask a friend over and brainstorm ideas for thinking kindly!

What I did:

What happened:

How I felt:

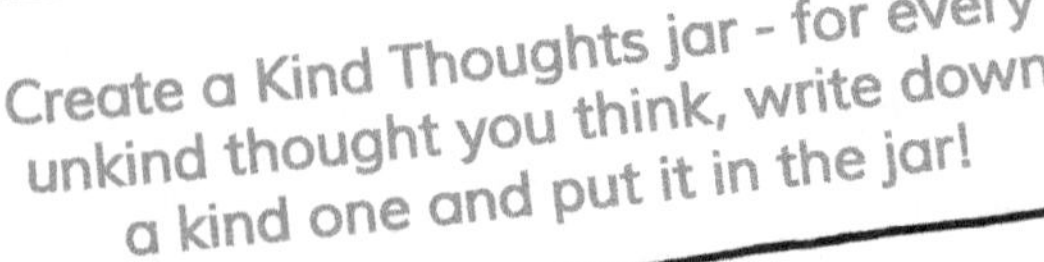

What I did:

What happened:

How I felt:

What I did:

What happened:

How I felt:

 loveandkindnessproject.org

Make up a Kind Thoughts rhyme and say it during times of stress!

What I did: _______________________________
____

What happened: _______________________________
____

How I felt: _______________________________
____
____

Remember a situation in which someone treated you kindly.

What I did: _______________________________
____

What happened: _______________________________
____

How I felt: _______________________________
____

What I did:

What happened:

How I felt:

What I did:

What happened:

How I felt:

 loveandkindnessproject.org

Take your dog for a walk and pay attention to how much they enjoy it!

What I did:

What happened:

How I felt:

Cuddle a cat!

What I did:

What happened:

How I felt:

What I did:

What happened:

How I felt:

What I did:

What happened:

How I felt:

   loveandkindnessproject.org

What I did:

What happened:

How I felt:

What I did:

What happened:

How I felt:

What I did:

What happened:

How I felt:

What I did:

What happened:

How I felt:

loveandkindnessproject.org

Start a Positive Thinking Group at work!

What I did: ___________________________________

____

What happened: _______________________________

____

How I felt: ___________________________________

____

____

Accept yourself for who you are!
You are just who you should be!

What I did: ___________________________________

____

What happened: _______________________________

____

How I felt: ___________________________________

____

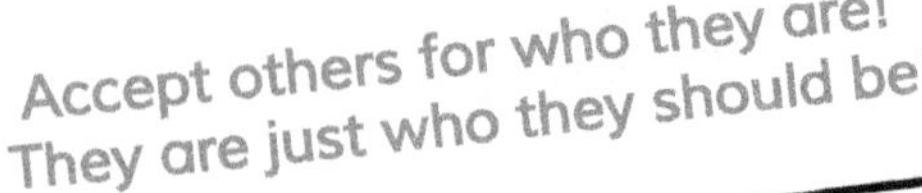

What I did:

What happened:

How I felt:

Make a list of everything you do.
Then write a positive statement
about each thing.

What I did:

What happened:

How I felt:

     loveandkindnessproject.org

Don't expect perfection!

What I did:

What happened:

How I felt:

Meditate!

What I did:

What happened:

How I felt:

Make a list of everything you
admire about your colleagues!

What I did:

What happened:

How I felt:

Make a list of everything you
admire about your partner!

What I did:

What happened:

How I felt:

   loveandkindnessproject.org

What I did:

What happened:

How I felt:

What I did:

What happened:

How I felt:

What I did:

What happened:

How I felt:

What I did:

What happened:

How I felt:

loveandkindnessproject.org

What I did:

What happened:

How I felt:

What I did:

What happened:

How I felt:

Make a 30 second video of you
saying a positive thought!

What I did:

What happened:

How I felt:

Put sticky notes with positive
quotes all around your cubicle!

What I did:

What happened:

How I felt:

loveandkindnessproject.org

Doodle hearts and smiley
faces on a sticky note!

What I did:

What happened:

How I felt:

Start your day by searching
for a positive quote on the internet!

What I did:

What happened:

How I felt:

What I did:

What happened:

How I felt:

What I did:

What happened:

How I felt:

 loveandkindnessproject.org

What I did:

What happened:

How I felt:

What I did:

What happened:

How I felt:

What I did:

What happened:

How I felt:

What I did:

What happened:

How I felt:

> Don't take what people say 'personally'!

What I did:

What happened:

How I felt:

> Go to bed earlier to get more sleep!

What I did:

What happened:

How I felt:

Cry! Let the bad feelings out!

What I did:

What happened:

How I felt:

Wear your favorite outfit!

What I did:

What happened:

How I felt:

 loveandkindnessproject.org

Spend a day 'walking in the shoes' of someone you don't get along with.

What I did:

What happened:

How I felt:

Take a micro-break!

What I did:

What happened:

How I felt:

What I did:
____

What happened:
____

How I felt:
____
____

What I did:
____

What happened:
____

How I felt:
____

loveandkindnessproject.org

What I did:

____

____

What happened:

____

____

How I felt:

____

____

____

What I did:

____

____

What happened:

____

____

How I felt:

____

____

Go outside in the rain and
splash in a puddle!

What I did:

What happened:

How I felt:

Write a list of nice things
you've done for people!

What I did:

What happened:

How I felt:

loveandkindnessproject.org

Write a list of all the things you thought you wouldn't be able to do...but did!

What I did:

What happened:

How I felt:

Think about a time you've surprised yourself in a good way!

What I did:

What happened:

How I felt:

What I did:

What happened:

How I felt:

What I did:

What happened:

How I felt:

loveandkindnessproject.org

Don't say 'I'm trying'...say
'I'm working on it' instead!

What I did:

What happened:

How I felt:

Make a list of all the reasons you think 'you
can't', then brainstorm ways you could!

What I did:

What happened:

How I felt:

What I did: _______________________
____

What happened: ___________________
____

How I felt: _______________________
____
____

What I did: _______________________
____

What happened: ___________________
____

How I felt: _______________________
____

    loveandkindnessproject.org

Keep a glass on your desk at work to remind yourself that 'the glass is always half-full'!

What I did:

What happened:

How I felt:

Share a kind thought every evening at dinner!

What I did:

What happened:

How I felt:

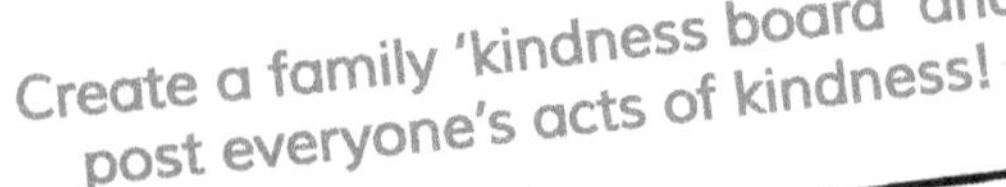

What I did:

What happened:

How I felt:

What I did:

What happened:

How I felt:

loveandkindnessproject.org

What I did: _______________________

____

What happened: _______________________

____

How I felt: _______________________

____

____

What I did: _______________________

____

What happened: _______________________

____

How I felt: _______________________

____

Challenge yourself to write down
twenty positive words!

What I did:

What happened:

How I felt:

Look up at the clouds and
picture fun shapes!

What I did:

What happened:

How I felt:

  loveandkindnessproject.org

Draw a picture of sunshine and flowers!

What I did: ___________________________
____

What happened: _______________________
____

How I felt: __________________________
____
____

Think about the 'best possible outcome', not the worst one!

What I did: ___________________________
____

What happened: _______________________
____

How I felt: __________________________
____
____

Take a shower and wash your negative thoughts down the drain!

What I did:

What happened:

How I felt:

Doodle with fun colored markers!

What I did:

What happened:

How I felt:

loveandkindnessproject.org

Write yourself a thank you note for acting kindly in a negative situation!

What I did:

What happened:

How I felt:

Start a 'Kind Thoughts Bank' at work! Have people put a kind thought in...and have people pull one out when they need it!

What I did:

What happened:

How I felt:

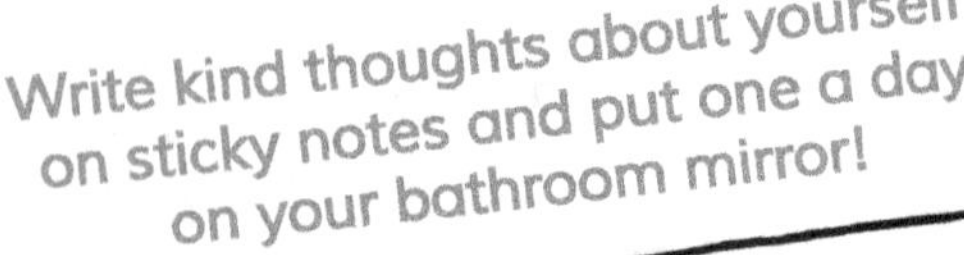

What I did:

What happened:

How I felt:

What I did:

What happened:

How I felt:

     loveandkindnessproject.org

Arrange to send positive texts with a friend throughout the day!

What I did:

What happened:

How I felt:

Write kind thoughts on sticky notes and put them on mirrors in public places places!

What I did:

What happened:

How I felt:

Use a picture that makes you feel positive as a screensaver on your phone!

What I did:

What happened:

How I felt:

Sign up for a site that sends you a positive thought each day!

What I did:

What happened:

How I felt:

loveandkindnessproject.org

Use a positive quote as a
screensaver on your computer!

What I did:

What happened:

How I felt:

Start your workday by sharing a story
of kindness with your team at work!

What I did:

What happened:

How I felt:

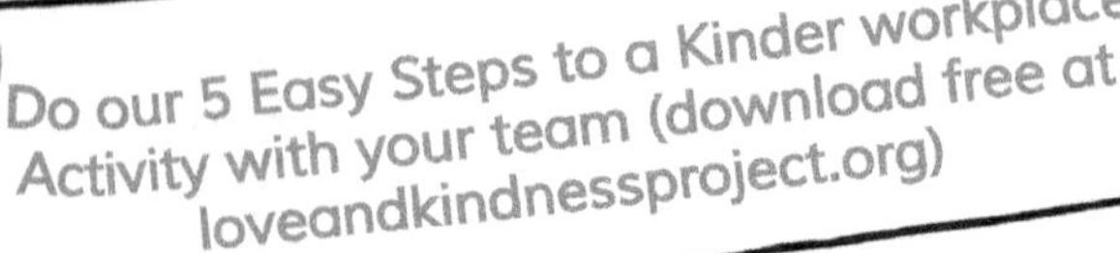

What I did: ___________________________

____

What happened: ________________________

____

How I felt: ___________________________

____

____

Eat healthier foods!

What I did: ___________________________

____

What happened: ________________________

____

How I felt: ___________________________

____

____

What I did:

What happened:

How I felt:

What I did:

What happened:

How I felt:

SPEAK KINDLY

Our words influence our actions
and create the world around us...

 loveandkindnessproject.org

What I did:

What happened:

How I felt:

What I did:

What happened:

How I felt:

What I did: ___________________________

____

What happened: ___________________________

____

How I felt: ___________________________

____

____

What I did: ___________________________

____

What happened: ___________________________

____

How I felt: ___________________________

____

What I did: _______________________________________

____

What happened: _______________________________

____

How I felt: _______________________________________

____

____

What I did: _______________________________________

____

What happened: _______________________________

____

How I felt: _______________________________________

____

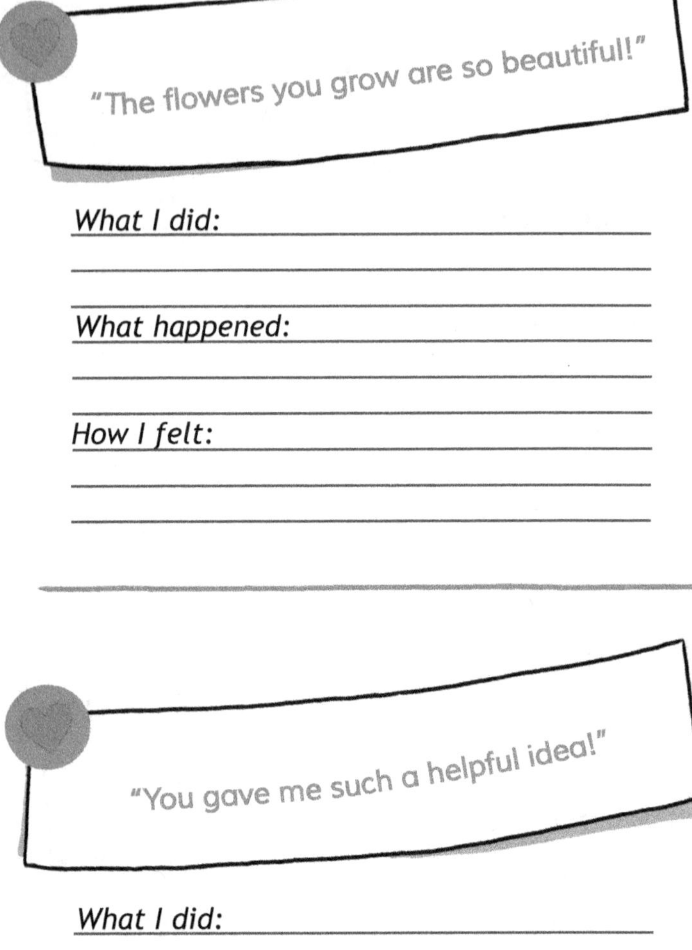

   loveandkindnessproject.org

"It's a pleasure being with you!"

What I did: _______________________

____

What happened: _______________________

____

How I felt: _______________________

____

____

"Thank you for offering to help me!"

What I did: _______________________

____

What happened: _______________________

____

How I felt: _______________________

____

____

"You're a great friend!"

What I did: ___________________________
____

What happened: _______________________
____

How I felt: __________________________
____
____

"You are so courageous!"

What I did: ___________________________
____

What happened: _______________________
____

How I felt: __________________________
____

loveandkindnessproject.org

"That was such a great effort!"

What I did: _______________________
____

What happened: ____________________
____

How I felt: ________________________
____
____

"How can I make your day better?"

What I did: _______________________
____

What happened: ____________________
____

How I felt: ________________________
____

> **"I love you!"**

What I did: _______________________

____

What happened: _______________________

____

How I felt: _______________________

____

____

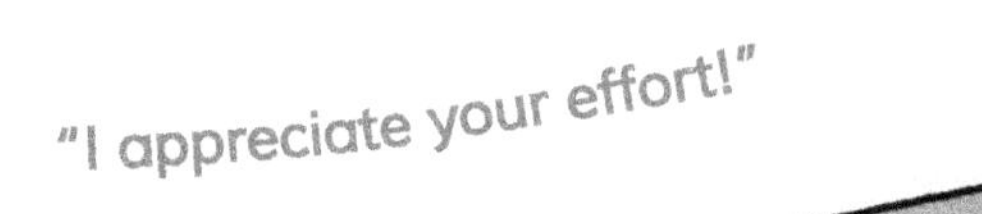

What I did: _______________________

____

What happened: _______________________

____

How I felt: _______________________

____

____

   loveandkindnessproject.org

"How can I help?!"

What I did:

What happened:

How I felt:

"Great job!"

What I did:

What happened:

How I felt:

"I'm so proud of you!"

What I did:

What happened:

How I felt:

"I'm brave!"

What I did:

What happened:

How I felt:

loveandkindnessproject.org

What I did: _______________________________

____

What happened: _______________________________

____

How I felt: _______________________________

____

____

What I did: _______________________________

____

What happened: _______________________________

____

How I felt: _______________________________

____

"I'm a great problem-solver!"

What I did: _______________________________
____

What happened: ___________________________
____

How I felt: _______________________________
____
____

"I really care about other people!"

What I did: _______________________________
____

What happened: ___________________________
____

How I felt: _______________________________
____

loveandkindnessproject.org

> **"I'm so patient!"**

What I did: ___________________________

____

What happened: _______________________

____

How I felt: ___________________________

____

____

> **"I really care about me!"**

What I did: ___________________________

____

What happened: _______________________

____

How I felt: ___________________________

____

"Spending time with you is a joy!"

What I did:

What happened:

How I felt:

"Everything is going to be okay."

What I did:

What happened:

How I felt:

  loveandkindnessproject.org

"I'm a great listener!"

What I did:

What happened:

How I felt:

"I have a great sense of humor!"

What I did:

What happened:

How I felt:

"I appreciate your suggestion!"

What I did:

What happened:

How I felt:

"I love myself for who I am!"

What I did:

What happened:

How I felt:

loveandkindnessproject.org

What I did: _______________________

____

What happened: _______________________

____

How I felt: _______________________

____

____

What I did: _______________________

____

What happened: _______________________

____

How I felt: _______________________

____

____

"I enjoy trying new things!"

What I did:

What happened:

How I felt:

"Help me to understand you better."

What I did:

What happened:

How I felt:

loveandkindnessproject.org

What I did: _______________________

____

What happened: _______________________

____

How I felt: _______________________

____

____

What I did: _______________________

____

What happened: _______________________

____

How I felt: _______________________

____

____

What I did:

What happened:

How I felt:

"Thanks for helping me think that through!"

What I did:

What happened:

How I felt:

loveandkindnessproject.org

What I did:

What happened:

How I felt:

What I did:

What happened:

How I felt:

"I look great today!"

What I did:

What happened:

How I felt:

"You're fabulous!"

What I did:

What happened:

How I felt:

 loveandkindnessproject.org

> "I'm so happy you are my friend!"

What I did: ___________________________
____

What happened: ________________________
____

How I felt: ___________________________
____
____

> "I'm fabulous!"

What I did: ___________________________
____

What happened: ________________________
____

How I felt: ___________________________
____

"You rock!"

What I did:

What happened:

How I felt:

"You're the best!"

What I did:

What happened:

How I felt:

loveandkindnessproject.org

"Congratulations!"

What I did: ______________________________
____

What happened: ___________________________
____

How I felt: ______________________________
____
____

"Thanks for such great advice!"

What I did: ______________________________
____

What happened: ___________________________
____

How I felt: ______________________________
____
____

"What can I do to cheer you up?"

What I did:

What happened:

How I felt:

"I really enjoy being around you!"

What I did:

What happened:

How I felt:

loveandkindnessproject.org

> *"Thank you for being my friend!"*

What I did:

What happened:

How I felt:

> *"I am special!"*

What I did:

What happened:

How I felt:

"When you ________
it makes me so happy!"

What I did:

What happened:

How I felt:

"I'm glad you're in my life,
because________."

What I did:

What happened:

How I felt:

loveandkindnessproject.org

> *"I'm glad you are my friend because ________!"*

What I did: ______________________________

____

What happened: __________________________

____

How I felt: _______________________________

____

____

> *"Thanks for being you!"*

What I did: ______________________________

____

What happened: __________________________

____

How I felt: _______________________________

____

"The world is a better place
because of you!"

What I did:

What happened:

How I felt:

"I really appreciate the time
you took to explain that to me."

What I did:

What happened:

How I felt:

     loveandkindnessproject.org

What I did: ___________________________
____

What happened: ___________________________
____

How I felt: ___________________________
____
____

What I did: ___________________________
____

What happened: ___________________________
____

How I felt: ___________________________
____

What I did:

What happened:

How I felt:

What I did:

What happened:

How I felt:

loveandkindnessproject.org

"It's okay. I know you didn't
do it on purpose."

What I did: _______________________________
____

What happened: ____________________________
____

How I felt: _______________________________
____
____

"I'm the helpful type!"

What I did: _______________________________
____

What happened: ____________________________
____

How I felt: _______________________________
____

> "That's alright!
> It was just an accident."

What I did: _______________________

____

What happened: ____________________

____

How I felt: _______________________

____

____

> "No one needs to be
> perfect! Including me!"

What I did: _______________________

____

What happened: ____________________

____

How I felt: _______________________

____

 loveandkindnessproject.org

"You don't have to be perfect. You're exactly who you are supposed to be!"

What I did:

What happened:

How I felt:

"That was really difficult!
And you didn't give up!"

What I did:

What happened:

How I felt:

"That was really difficult...
and I didn't give up!"

What I did:

What happened:

How I felt:

"I don't need to know how to do
something perfectly the first time I try it!"

What I did:

What happened:

How I felt:

    loveandkindnessproject.org

> **"I can think more positively!"**

What I did:

What happened:

How I felt:

> **"I can do difficult things."**

What I did:

What happened:

How I felt:

What I did:

What happened:

How I felt:

What I did:

What happened:

How I felt:

loveandkindnessproject.org

"I'm so glad we work together!"

What I did:

What happened:

How I felt:

"I just need some more practice!"

What I did:

What happened:

How I felt:

"What can I do to help?"

What I did: ____
____

What happened: ____
____

How I felt: ____
____
____

"I'm making such great progress!"

What I did: ____
____

What happened: ____
____

How I felt: ____
____

loveandkindnessproject.org

"I can always choose to be kind!"

What I did:

What happened:

How I felt:

"What can I do to make things better?"

What I did:

What happened:

How I felt:

What I did:

What happened:

How I felt:

What I did:

What happened:

How I felt:

 loveandkindnessproject.org

What I did: ______________________

____

What happened: ______________________

____

How I felt: ______________________

____

____

What I did: ______________________

____

What happened: ______________________

____

How I felt: ______________________

____

What I did:

What happened:

How I felt:

What I did:

What happened:

How I felt:

loveandkindnessproject.org

"I can try again tomorrow!"

What I did:

What happened:

How I felt:

"Don't worry! Everything will be alright!"

What I did:

What happened:

How I felt:

What I did: _______________________

____

What happened: _______________________

____

How I felt: _______________________

____

____

What I did: _______________________

____

What happened: _______________________

____

How I felt: _______________________

____

     loveandkindnessproject.org

> *"Tomorrow will be a better day!"*

What I did:

What happened:

How I felt:

> *"Thanks for cheering me up today."*

What I did:

What happened:

How I felt:

What I did: ___________________________
____

What happened: ________________________
____

How I felt: ___________________________
____
____

What I did: ___________________________
____

What happened: ________________________
____

How I felt: ___________________________
____

    loveandkindnessproject.org

"I'm happy to give you a
hand if you'd like!"

What I did:

What happened:

How I felt:

"There's a rainbow on the way!"

What I did:

What happened:

How I felt:

> "You did the best you could!"

What I did:

What happened:

How I felt:

> "You're so important to me!"

What I did:

What happened:

How I felt:

   loveandkindnessproject.org

> "I appreciate your kind words!"

What I did: ___________________________

____

What happened: _______________________

____

How I felt: ___________________________

____

____

> "I know you did your very best!"

What I did: ___________________________

____

What happened: _______________________

____

How I felt: ___________________________

____

What I did:

____

What happened:

____

How I felt:

____

____

What I did:

____

What happened:

____

How I felt:

____

    loveandkindnessproject.org

> *"You can do more than
> you think you can!"*

What I did: _______________________________

____

What happened: ___________________________

____

How I felt: ________________________________

____

____

> *"I've really put in the effort to improve!"*

What I did: _______________________________

____

What happened: ___________________________

____

How I felt: ________________________________

____

____

What I did: ___________________________
____

What happened: ___________________________
____

How I felt: ___________________________
____
____

What I did: ___________________________
____

What happened: ___________________________
____

How I felt: ___________________________
____

loveandkindnessproject.org

"I'm in a great place!"

What I did:

What happened:

How I felt:

"You're so kind!"

What I did:

What happened:

How I felt:

"You did it!"

What I did: _______________________________
____
____

What happened: ___________________________
____

How I felt: _______________________________
____
____

"I did it!"

What I did: _______________________________
____

What happened: ___________________________
____

How I felt: _______________________________
____
____

loveandkindnessproject.org

"I love it that you are so thoughtful!"

What I did: ______________________________

____

What happened: ______________________________

____

How I felt: ______________________________

____

____

"I admire how you are always willing to try!"

What I did: ______________________________

____

What happened: ______________________________

____

How I felt: ______________________________

____

____

What I did: _______________________

____

What happened: _______________________

____

How I felt: _______________________

____

____

What I did: _______________________

____

What happened: _______________________

____

How I felt: _______________________

____

loveandkindnessproject.org

> "It's not easy to change,
> but it's worth it!"

What I did: _______________________________________

____

What happened: _______________________________________

____

How I felt: _______________________________________

____

____

> "I can persevere!"

What I did: _______________________________________

____

What happened: _______________________________________

____

How I felt: _______________________________________

____

What I did: _______________________

____

What happened: _______________________

____

How I felt: _______________________

____

____

What I did: _______________________

____

What happened: _______________________

____

How I felt: _______________________

____

   loveandkindnessproject.org

> *"Being kind to myself is as important as being kind to others!"*

What I did: _______________________________

____

What happened: _______________________________

____

How I felt: _______________________________

____

____

> *"Thanks for doing this with me!"*

What I did: _______________________________

____

What happened: _______________________________

____

How I felt: _______________________________

____

____

ACT KINDLY

Our actions create our thoughts...

 loveandkindnessproject.org

What I did:

What happened:

How I felt:

What I did:

What happened:

How I felt:

What I did:

What happened:

How I felt:

What I did:

What happened:

How I felt:

loveandkindnessproject.org

Give up your seat on the bus
for someone!

What I did: ___________________________________

____

What happened: _______________________________

____

How I felt: ___________________________________

____

____

If you are in an aisle seat on a plane,
and a taller person has the seat next to
you, offer to change seats!

What I did: ___________________________________

____

What happened: _______________________________

____

How I felt: ___________________________________

____

____

What I did:

What happened:

How I felt:

What I did:

What happened:

How I felt:

 loveandkindnessproject.org

Strike up a conversation with someone in an elevator!

What I did:

What happened:

How I felt:

Donate unneeded pet toys, beds and bowls to an animal shelter!

What I did:

What happened:

How I felt:

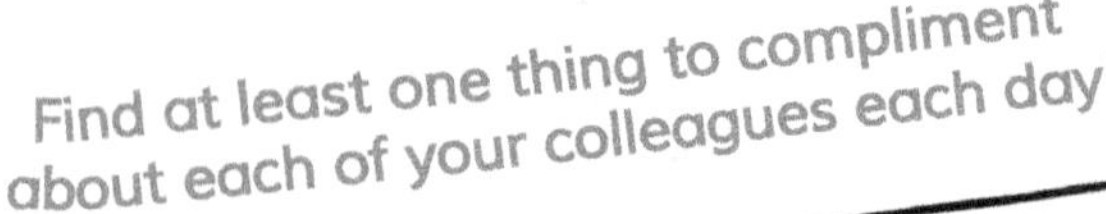

What I did:

What happened:

How I felt:

What I did:

What happened:

How I felt:

loveandkindnessproject.org

What I did:

What happened:

How I felt:

What I did:

What happened:

How I felt:

Say 'Thank you' to security guards!

What I did:

____

____

What happened:

____

____

How I felt:

____

____

____

Let someone else take the parking spot...
even if you think you saw it first!

What I did:

____

____

What happened:

____

____

How I felt:

____

____

loveandkindnessproject.org

Ask the cashier and person packing
your groceries how they are today!
Then listen to their answers!

What I did:

What happened:

How I felt:

Smile at everyone!

What I did:

What happened:

How I felt:

Help an elderly person put
their groceries in their car!

What I did:

What happened:

How I felt:

Let your neighbor's dogs out if they
are going to be home late!

What I did:

What happened:

How I felt:

loveandkindnessproject.org

Call someone you haven't
spoken to in a while!

What I did:

What happened:

How I felt:

Pick up groceries for your elderly
neighbor while you do your shopping!

What I did:

What happened:

How I felt:

What I did:

What happened:

How I felt:

What I did:

What happened:

How I felt:

　loveandkindnessproject.org

Turn off your phone and/or computer
and play with your kids and/or pets!

What I did:

What happened:

How I felt:

Clean up a park or
neighborhood common space!

What I did:

What happened:

How I felt:

What I did:

What happened:

How I felt:

What I did:

What happened:

How I felt:

loveandkindnessproject.org

Create a relaxing environment
for someone who is going
through a stressful time.

What I did:

What happened:

How I felt:

Lend someone your umbrella!

What I did:

What happened:

How I felt:

What I did:

What happened:

How I felt:

What I did:

What happened:

How I felt:

 loveandkindnessproject.org

Ask a homeless person their name and have a conversation with them!

What I did: ___________________________
____

What happened: _______________________
____

How I felt: ___________________________
____
____

Call your dad!

What I did: ___________________________
____

What happened: _______________________
____

How I felt: ___________________________
____

What I did:

What happened:

How I felt:

What I did:

What happened:

How I felt:

 loveandkindnessproject.org

Visit a nursing home and spend time with someone you don't know!

What I did:

What happened:

How I felt:

Compliment everyone you pass by!

What I did:

What happened:

How I felt:

What I did:

What happened:

How I felt:

What I did:

What happened:

How I felt:

loveandkindnessproject.org

Wish the barista at your local coffee shop a good day!

What I did:

What happened:

How I felt:

Bring a family member a snack!

What I did:

What happened:

How I felt:

Unload the dishwasher...
even though it's not 'your job'!

What I did:

What happened:

How I felt:

Give someone one of your reusable
bags if they don't have one!

What I did:

What happened:

How I felt:

loveandkindnessproject.org

What I did:

What happened:

How I felt:

What I did:

What happened:

How I felt:

What I did:

What happened:

How I felt:

What I did:

What happened:

How I felt:

loveandkindnessproject.org

What I did:

What happened:

How I felt:

What I did:

What happened:

How I felt:

Carry your own water-bottle!

What I did:

What happened:

How I felt:

Give extra school supplies to a school - or child - in need!

What I did:

What happened:

How I felt:

loveandkindnessproject.org

Help your kids make friendship bracelets to give to EVERYONE in their class!

What I did:

What happened:

How I felt:

Hold the door for someone!

What I did:

What happened:

How I felt:

Vacuum the house!

What I did:

What happened:

How I felt:

Bring a board game to a senior citizens home and play with the residents!

What I did:

What happened:

How I felt:

loveandkindnessproject.org

Look around and hold
the elevator for someone!

What I did:

What happened:

How I felt:

Hug someone!

What I did:

What happened:

How I felt:

Give an old blanket you have
to a homeless person!

What I did:

What happened:

How I felt:

Shovel your neighbor's
walkway if it snows!

What I did:

What happened:

How I felt:

   loveandkindnessproject.org

Help someone get something
from a high - or low - shelf!

What I did:

____

What happened:

____

How I felt:

____

____

Rake your neighbor's leaves!

What I did:

____

What happened:

____

How I felt:

____

Repair a broken toy or stuffed animal!

What I did:

What happened:

How I felt:

Turn something you've found
into Lost and Found!

What I did:

What happened:

How I felt:

   loveandkindnessproject.org

Pick up something someone
has dropped and give it to them!

What I did:

What happened:

How I felt:

Give an outgrown bicycle to a
neighborhood family in need!

What I did:

What happened:

How I felt:

Offer to do your brother or sister's laundry!

What I did:

What happened:

How I felt:

Send a hand-written thank you note!

What I did:

What happened:

How I felt:

 loveandkindnessproject.org

Give books you aren't reading
anymore to a homeless shelter!

What I did:

What happened:

How I felt:

Write a positive review on social media!

What I did:

What happened:

How I felt:

Write an "I forgive you" note to someone.

What I did:

What happened:

How I felt:

Call someone and apologize for something you did that might have hurt their feelings.

What I did:

What happened:

How I felt:

loveandkindnessproject.org

Give a hand-written thank you note to person who takes away your trash!

What I did:

What happened:

How I felt:

Take your neighbor's trash cans in for them!

What I did:

What happened:

How I felt:

Clap for someone!

What I did:

What happened:

How I felt:

Stop working and play a board game with your kids!

What I did:

What happened:

How I felt:

loveandkindnessproject.org

Leave an anonymous note with a kind thought for a friend or family member!

What I did:

What happened:

How I felt:

Send someone a link to an article you read that made you think of them!

What I did:

What happened:

How I felt:

What I did: _______________________

____

What happened: _______________________

____

How I felt: _______________________

____

____

What I did: _______________________

____

What happened: _______________________

____

How I felt: _______________________

____

loveandkindnessproject.org

Take the stairs! It's kind to your health!

What I did:

What happened:

How I felt:

Clean the house – even if it's not your turn!

What I did:

What happened:

How I felt:

Listen without interrupting!

What I did: ____

____

What happened: ____

____

How I felt: ____

____

____

Don't complain about anyONE for a whole day!

What I did: ____

____

What happened: ____

____

How I felt: ____

____

 loveandkindnessproject.org

> Don't complain about anyTHING
> for a whole day!

What I did: _________________________

____

What happened: _________________________

____

How I felt: _________________________

____

____

> Write an email to a friend
> in another country!

What I did: _________________________

____

What happened: _________________________

____

How I felt: _________________________

____

What I did: _______________________________

____

What happened: _______________________________

____

How I felt: _______________________________

____

____

What I did: _______________________________

____

What happened: _______________________________

____

How I felt: _______________________________

____

loveandkindnessproject.org

Go to a free concert with someone who wants to go but doesn't have anyone to go with!

What I did:

What happened:

How I felt:

Help a friend move apartments!

What I did:

What happened:

How I felt:

What I did:

What happened:

How I felt:

What I did:

What happened:

How I felt:

   loveandkindnessproject.org

Say 'good morning' to the person sitting next to you even if you don't know them!

What I did:

What happened:

How I felt:

Transport a rescue dog or cat!

What I did:

What happened:

How I felt:

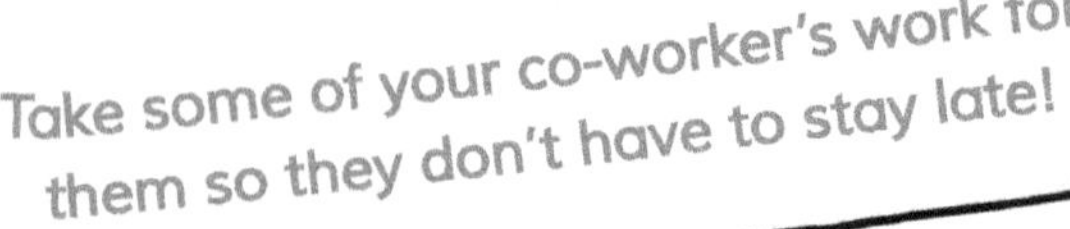

What I did:

What happened:

How I felt:

What I did:

What happened:

How I felt:

 loveandkindnessproject.org

Drive an elderly person to their social group or place of worship!

What I did:

What happened:

How I felt:

Write thank you notes to your co-workers for times they've helped you!

What I did:

What happened:

How I felt:

What I did:

____

____

What happened:

____

____

How I felt:

____

____

____

What I did:

____

____

What happened:

____

____

How I felt:

____

____

     loveandkindnessproject.org

Mail a letter for someone!

What I did: _______________________

____

What happened: ___________________

____

How I felt: _______________________

____

____

Give someone a Love and Kindness Button!

What I did: _______________________

____

What happened: ___________________

____

How I felt: _______________________

____

____

Help clean up a spilled drink!

What I did:

What happened:

How I felt:

Change tables in a restaurant so a
large group can sit together!

What I did:

What happened:

How I felt:

     loveandkindnessproject.org

Clean up the dishes in the sink at work
- no matter whose they are!

What I did:

What happened:

How I felt:

Help someone pump up their bicycle tires!

What I did:

What happened:

How I felt:

Help clean out the garage or attic!

What I did:

What happened:

How I felt:

Fill out a survey with a positive response!

What I did:

What happened:

How I felt:

loveandkindnessproject.org

Recycle!

What I did:

What happened:

How I felt:

Compost!

What I did:

What happened:

How I felt:

Make silly faces with the kids
in the line at the store.

What I did:

What happened:

How I felt:

Cook dinner for your friends.

What I did:

What happened:

How I felt:

loveandkindnessproject.org

Offer to drive!

What I did: _______________________________
____

What happened: ___________________________
____

How I felt: ______________________________
____
____

Mentor a kid.

What I did: _______________________________
____

What happened: ___________________________
____

How I felt: ______________________________
____

Make something yummy and share
it with people at work!

What I did:

What happened:

How I felt:

Share or like a post on social media
to help out a friend's small business.

What I did:

What happened:

How I felt:

          loveandkindnessproject.org

What I did:

What happened:

How I felt:

What I did:

What happened:

How I felt:

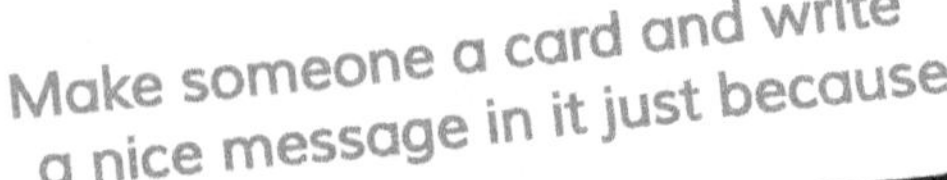

What I did:

What happened:

How I felt:

What I did:

What happened:

How I felt:

     loveandkindnessproject.org

Bring someone soup
when they are sick.

What I did:

What happened:

How I felt:

Make time for someone
especially if you are "too busy."

What I did:

What happened:

How I felt:

Now that you have completed your
kindness practice, what should you do?

START AGAIN!

Because being kind is an ongoing -
and endless - practice!

And if you have ideas on how to think, speak
and act kindly, send them to us!
We will use them to create next year's edition:
admin@loveandkindnessproject.org.

www.ingramcontent.com/pod-product-compliance
Lightning Source LLC
Chambersburg PA
CBHW071416150726
48000CB00001B/344